C000205448

Scribbles of a Broken Sparrow

By
Jami Lyne Kellett

Copyright © 2021 Jami Lyne Kellett
All Rights Reserved

ISBN: 978-0-578-86611-6

Dedicated to my husband:

You saved me from myself.
I'll always be indebted to you for
bringing joy back into my life.

To my children:

I needed you more than you needed me.

To my family:

I love all of you.
I cannot put into words how much.

This collection of poems are words from my soul.
Writing has been a way for me to heal from depression and
anxiety.

I hope this book resonates with you in some way -
not to bring sadness, but a validation of feelings.

My wish is that you feel a sense of hope,
that there is light at the end of the tunnel.

You can get better and feel better.
There is joy in this world.

Choose life every time, you won't regret it.

Perhaps we are jealous of the birds,
their freedom to soar to the open sky

We ourselves captured by immense
lack of reciprocity and predicament,
feeling trapped in our own world,
caged with the door left slightly open

Fluttering and floundering in the small space,
the bird anticipates his release
for he knows he's destined to soar
up to the heavens

A human who knows his worth
anticipates the release from his circumstance,
for there's more to life
than this small cage

Open the door mere human and fly,
soar past your circumstance
past this caged life you've endured.

Reach for the sky, believe you can fly,
immeasurable potential within you-
open the door and soar.

This body is a vessel in which I go through life.

My physical scars and imperfections apparent,
a shell of who I am.

Rather, capture a portrait of my soul.

Every sunset I have ever seen casts
light on the turmoil and chaos that reside there.

Love fills the void the darkness left behind.

Dear Anxiety:

I think you've caused enough fear and
uncertainty in my life.

The roller coaster of events,
so much time wasted and spent.

Can we stop this shit?

-Me.

Late in the night and you feel all alone
the pain of the past comes
knocking on your heart's door,
you know you can't let it in

Tears flow ...

you've been down this road before

this too shall pass
tomorrow will be better
there's hope.

*The mountains are high
the valleys are green and low
wonder, awe and peace abound.*

--

*I long for silence,
to walk in the forest
and*

just be.

He played my heart like a violin,
my body like a symphony; and
my soul like a concerto.

In perfect tempo-

the music we made
was quite the performance, but
the standing ovation was to be applauded.

Standing before you
with
tears in my eyes

--watching you go--

You found another.

You say you don't love me, yet
you were the air that I breathed.

You promised me forever
under the night sky.

With a ring in your hand
you gave your heart and
left mine barren.

I crawled straight out of hell,
--stood up--
and
fought the demons within me.

Depression may have tried to kill me, but
it didn't break my spirit and my will to survive.

In your eyes, I may appear weak.

Don't mistake me for weak,
I'm far from it.

Amidst the silence, internally screaming
--longing to be heard--

--

Many times in my life
I felt invisible.

My mind was playing
tricks on me.

Two souls engulfed and entangled
left gasping for air.

Igniting a fire
hearts ablaze
desperate and wanting.

Searching for water
from the oceans to the sea
to quench their thirst.

Reaching to the depths
of the earth to find their reprise.

You are one in a million.

*There is not a single soul like
you on this earth.*

You are irreplaceable!

~You are valued and you are loved ~

I'm tired, my soul weary,
somewhat lost and broken

As the tears steam down my face,
I will hold my head up high and
not feel defeated.

I know victory is around the corner.

In other words, I'm fine.

Your feelings are valid;
not something to
be put upon a shelf and forgotten.

You are heard.
You matter.
You are enough.

At the end of this life,
we've had both
joy and tragedy.

No one leaves
this earth unscathed.

Every day,
day in and day out
there are sacrifices to be made:
kids, mortgage and bills.

We decided to stay and
do this life.

Each putting forth the effort to
build this family that we've made.

To make this home a happy one -
through love & admiration,
we've done it together.

There's peace on the other side of the storm
where time has healed the wounds.

The clouds are lifting,
silently revealing
love and light.

Stay strong while you weather the storm;
brighter days are ahead.

*All my thoughts that I need to survive are
neatly tucked away within my mind.*

*Strewn to the side are the empty boxes,
once filled with sadness and despair.*

*This depression desperately
wants to fill them back up again.*

I refuse.

This year has been difficult for me,
yet I learned a lot about myself:

I learned to slow down
I learned that I cannot
control some things in my life.

I do know this:
I love this home and everything in it.

The time spent with my family,
I wouldn't have otherwise had.

I am blessed.

Walking through life unsuspecting

absence of spirit,
a shell of one's self

carrying the world on two shoulders
no one would suspect, unless revealed ...

Unrelenting sadness
most
would fear.

Happy face
with
no complaints.

--

Taking little bits and pieces along the way,
depression
wills you to wither and decay.

As a writer, I question my talent:

*I have a story within my heart that
bleeds onto the pages as it flows deep within
my soul.*

*Persistence becomes a gift,
a reward to myself in bringing it to fruition ...
from soul to paper.*

*Listening to the rain fall
it is otherwise quiet.*

*Can I be alone in this moment-
to enjoy existing, breathing
to feel my heart beating?*

*My muscles relax, yet
my mind has awakened to
chaos and past memories.*

*Silence has stirred and
I ... it's victim.*

You are the anchor that grounds me,
yet gives me space to flow.

Through torrential rain,
we weather the storm.

Our refuge is the solace found
under a starry night in each other's arms.

Tethered together in a breakable bond
drifting through the sea of life.

I've often wondered why some people
have to endure so much pain in their lives,
the unfairness and dissolution of happiness and joy.

I realized that somehow, an
inner strength is found deep inside.

A strength that would otherwise lay dormant.

Sometimes in life you think you're
not strong enough for the struggle,
but you are.

Keep going.
Keep fighting.

Believe in yourself today!
Hold your head up high.
Keep smiling.
Count your blessings.
Life is a beautiful thing.
You really are worth it.

You are deserving of beautiful
things and all that life brings.

My days numbered,
cast in a proverbial hat
for
the Master to draw one eventful day.

Lonely one night, I pulled my number
and I laid in slumber
just the Master and me.

I awakened reborn with the joy of life,
its beauty and grace.

He whispered, "It's not your time."

I never wanted to be like everyone else.

I talk about feelings: deep, dark ones -
mental illness, depression and suicide.

I also talk about love, peace
and understanding.

Uncomfortable for some,
but I want to normalize those conversations
and create a safe haven for others
to talk openly, without judgment.

A bride walks down the aisle to marry,
her beloved's heart she did carry.

Guests in awe of what they saw.
The groom stood in wait,
tears down his face.

A house is only brick and mortar,
she was his home and he adored her.

If walls could talk, they would say-
it was clear that love lived here.

I've been anxious.
I've been depressed.
I need to yank myself out of this mess.

*Many times, I've waited the entire night
for just a glimpse of the morning light.
It's a promise to me that there's hope.*

*I have faith that regardless
of what is going on in my life,
the sun will rise bringing forth a new day.*

There's joy in life, look up.

*I am living proof that you can
survive suicidal thoughts.*

*I am alive today
because someone cared.*

*My determination to get
better and survive wasn't
always about me, but it is now.*

Choose life, you won't regret it.

Sending you:

Strength: to face whatever comes your way

Love: a reminder of your significance in this world

Peace: to calm any doubts you may have.

*It must be the anxiety
keeping me up at night,
the overthinking is insane
worrying about everything.*

*Not being able to control
the situations in my life –*

*I'm in the back seat,
fighting to get up front
to hit the brakes - because
the car is swerving out of control.*

Self-doubt
Overthinking
Smothering
Unable to breathe
Gasping for air
Incapacitated
Instantaneous panic

Tethered between the body and mind-
there is no escape from one's own self.

I cry out to the heavens as I cannot comprehend
the suffering of so many
Summer
Spring
Winter
Fall, that seems to be where we are
falling as a society:

sickness, homelessness,
the economy and despair -
crippling us as a people.

The whys and the pleas are not coming to me.

Broken branches and
fractured hearts

Torn and stripped
of their beauty

Discarded like the
others before it

Pieces that cannot
be replaced

Standing tall,
yet falling apart

Repairing the scars
and attempt to heal

To find a sense of
normalcy, to move on.

I pour my heart out for all the world to see
my emotions on display while others cause dismay

Does anyone notice the sacrifice
I bare for sharing bits and pieces of myself out there?

My fears and bottled up tears in an open book
for all to have ... just a little look.

In the midst of life,
I've lost myself.

With everyone watching,
yet no one can see the
emotions swirling around in me.

My identity shrouded,
my needs seem clouded.

Who am I anymore?

Sacrifice, life on hold
Standing still while years pass by
Take a backseat, while another drives
Overwhelming responsibilities
Stuck between what you need
Trapped by what you love

*Hope leads the way for the
broken hearted and forgotten souls.*

*Hold on to hope,
it will lead you out of darkness
and into the light.*

-Anxiety and Insomnia -

*A state of panic as scenarios play
over and over.*

This mind wanders to the past.

*Caught in a never-ending battle of
tossing and turning.*

*Shorter days are
longer nights,
ending with the
morning light.*

*A tombstone inscribed with my name
is the only reminder left of me.*

*I should have been there,
my body under the tree for
all the world to see.*

*It wasn't my time and I
intend to leave this world,
a little better than when I came into it,
maybe then you'll remember me.*

I wrote these words in ink
as reminder of how far I've come and
to never forget where I've been.

A passage to my soul that is etched
upon my heart and carved within my mind.

A soul left broken and charred,
the embers slowly consuming.

Deep in a depressive hell,
a shell of blackness.

A sliver of hope amongst the wreckage,
a will to survive despite the pain.

Blistered & tattered,
all consuming,
yet all in.

Damaged, but alive and
I was the lucky one.

~*Wait Around*~

They say time is on your side,
but what if it's not?

Sickening reality of the
waiting game,
panic sets in and you're thinking
the worst, yet hoping for the best.

A 50/50 proposition.

Patience is a virtue
and
waiting induces anxiety.

Thoughts take me back
a million miles away
when time stood still
responsibilities scarce
expectations low.

Is it selfish to want to go back there?

for I've lost myself

I'm buried beneath
burdens and expectations.

Our hearts need love and comfort
Our souls, happiness and joy
Our minds, peace and balance

We need one another in times of need

If I stay, will I be your puppet on a string?
Get lost in someone else's dream?

My own identity shadowed by yours,
it shakes me to my very core.

My dreams washed up on the shore,
hope waning as you walk out the door.

I promised to be your wife in this life.

The stillness of the night
the darkness of a room.

Vulnerable and weak
questioning and pondering
overthinking and insomnia
fears and bottled up tears
the what-ifs and could-haves

-haunt me.

Sharing positivity and kindness
is planting a seed of goodness
in an uncertain and cynical world.

Love and compassion for one another
is providing the water and care
for that seed to take hold and flourish

Together we can grow from a garden of hope.

Bent beneath the weight of the world,
is too much to bear.

At times, it has become my plight in life.
I am strong and can carry my burdens.

My weakness is, I can't share.
I can't hand them off for you to bear,
everything dear to me is up there.

The clock is ticking
The pendulum to and fro
Days and weeks turn into years
Love and Loss
Happiness and heartache
Sunrise to Sunset
Beginning to end
It's precious
It's fleeting
It's life.

Her heart is gentle and pure,
despite its little dents.

Her soul magnified by her will and perseverance.

Survivor is written across her very being.

Giving up is not in her vocabulary.

*Missed opportunities due to
immense responsibilities,
life passes by.*

The river of life is forever flowing,
while serene and picturesque,
navigating through the unknown,
deep and dark waters lurk

The undertow is swift and untamed
pulling you into a suffocating abyss,
yet all you hear is a trickle.

Soft glow from the window:

As I open my eyes,
I lie here thinking that
it was only a dream

Yet, I know in my heart
it is reality.

The state before waking,
that's where I'll find you.

You are here and all is
right with the world.

Romance is not always candles and
rose petals scattered throughout a room.

Romance is a love strong enough
to weather life's storms.

A shelter to run to in times of need,
a promise of everlasting love and acceptance.

Romance is ... I am never going to leave you.

Love this life.

Our time is fleeting,
we are here for just a moment.

Love one another,
give grace to each other.

Be grateful for what you have.

Help one another,
there's no doubt that
your life will be enriched.

*Sometimes knowing you are not the
only one going through a tough time,
can make all the difference.*

*Remember:
You matter
You are not alone
You are loved
You are needed
You are not invisible
You are not your diagnosis
You can get better
Reach out.*

Take me to the ocean
with its soft breeze and
gentle seas,
because it's a part of me.

Tsunami fueled emotion,
waves crashing beyond the shore.

Catastrophic destruction,
earthquake below the surface.

Tears into the sea,
distained unity between the

heart
mind
body
and
soul
released.

I was his flower
his happily ever after
his "I can't live without you."

He stomped on my soul,
took my heart and threw it away.

Someone came along and
gently picked me up,
showed me how to love again,
how to live again.

Now, I'm his rose.

Trials, tribulations and
difficult circumstances.

Slowly, little by little,
a transformation
and healing.

Piece by piece pulled back,
hope emerges,
life is restored.

Fly butterfly, fly

Darkness tearing at my soul
like a thief in the night
stealing away happiness and joy.

A blanket smothering me with
doom, despair and injustice.

I long for a beacon of light
to cast a light on my soul,
for I am blinded by darkness,

Begging to be set free.

*I refuse to be a sacrificial lamb and
be impaled by the sword of my demons.*

*An inner war of conflict and duress,
filled with heartache.*

*I will face the battles of my enemy,
as a survivor and a warrior.*

The anger runs circles in my mind,
because I can't take it back.

There are some things in life
you can't take back.

Even though I was sick and
not in the right state of mind,
it pisses me off the things
you took from me.

Fuck you, depression.
Fuck you.

One story brought me to my knees,
all the past comes flooding back.

The mistakes, the pain and I feel it,
just like it happened that day.

What the hell, I would have left my kids!

What was I thinking?
Stop.
Give grace.

Think straight, I was sick.

My self-worth was dependent,
I need to be mended.

A need for perfection, as
I have no direction.

A fear of failure,
is my plight.

I try with all my might
to face these fears.

So many times, I felt locked inside,
feeling trapped in my own mind.

Holed up in an emotional prison,
the only escape is begging and pleading
to be set free from this inner turmoil.

Crawling from the depths of hell,
to save myself from the demon's spell.

Hand in hand in London they stroll,
many shoppes on this cobblestone street.

The wind picks up as they take it all in

Aroma from the pubs demand their attention,
they settle on a quaint pub, dim lighting.

They are getting acquainted

Fruit, the red wine and cheese please

He pulls his chair closer,
a wisp of hair across her face.

There's something special about this place

She gently parts her beautiful lips,
his hand falls upon her hips.

Falling in love.

I don't know your story,
or where you've been.

I can't read your mind,
or where to begin.

I don't know your struggle,
and when it ends.

No judgment, just compassion,
I can only imagine.

Your story
Your experiences
Your memories
Your heartache
Your pain
Your happiness

YOUR life
YOUR rules

*Wedding bells or
a partner that never fails.*

*The pitter patter of little feet or
the fur baby at your seat.*

*Friends that take you in or
the parent whose seen your sin.*

*Love and compassion,
acceptance and admiration.*

*Your anchor in rough waters,
family never falters.*

Two lovers walking on the sand,
he drops to one knee and takes her hand.

Will you be mine 'til the end of time?

For fifty years they've been blessed,
the magic of entwined lives.

As she slips away, he takes her hand -
Will you be mine, 'til the end of time?

You are beautiful
You are not your weight
You are not your circumstance
You are intelligent
You have big dreams
You have unimaginable potential

Keep these words in your heart today

Feeling invisible?
I see you over there trying your best
I see you putting forth the effort
I see you encouraging others
I see you struggling
I see you discouraged
I see you.

Sadness, darkness, despair
Happiness, faith, hope

Fatigued, exhausted, defeated
Strong, confident, accomplished

Worthlessness, empty, alone
Elated, ambition, clarity

Redirect your words, even if you
don't believe them right now.

*Survivors crawl from the depths of hell
to fight their demons to survive.*

*Sometimes, out of nowhere,
the demon comes back,
haunting them again and
they find themselves fighting
the same battle.*

*Don't forget you
are a survivor.*

*Stay strong.
Keep fighting.*

I realize that life is not always easy,
it can be difficult at times.

Remember, life can be good too.

Sometimes, it takes finding the little things
that is right in our lives, to see that it's not all bad.

Don't overlook the good things in life,
search for them if you have to.

At the end of the day,
life is about family and friends;
it's happiness and love that
they leave in our hearts.

I hope you feel love today.
If not, I'm sending you love.

I hope it warms your heart.

That day
That hour
That minute
Those pills
That pain
That past
What would I have missed?
These kids
That love
The memories
What have I learned?
Gratitude
Grace and
Goodness
Most importantly?
This life is my life.

Kindness
Love
Acceptance
Patience
Understanding

Is really what we all want in life.

I hope you feel them today.

You are my summer and my rain,
my days and my nights

Lying next to you,
I want into your slumber

Grab my hand and take
me into your dreams,
show me mystical things

For I dream no more
it's dark to the core

Take me into your dreams.

I'm ok to be alone and
I have never said that out loud
and it feels good.

A huge breakthrough.

In life,
sometimes
you soldier on
and
that's ok,
as long as you keep going.

By ourselves, we are weak -
together, we are fierce.

A soul broken in a million pieces.

~

Future of Impossibilities

~

Shell of Emptiness

~

*Rock bottom with nowhere
else to go but down*

~

Depression

~

Demons

~

Darkness

~

Help

~

Hope

~

Happiness

~

Love

~

Light

~

Patience

~

Peace.

I am bruised,
my soul tattered

Let the rain fall and
cleanse my spirit

As the thunder deafens the cries
let the wind blow through my very being,
releasing the difficulties from within

As lightening sparks across the sky,
let it shed light into my heart and
quench my weary soul.

Darkness begets darkness
a dark room, a dark mind
a dark heart, a dark soul

hour upon hour
night after night
you wait and you wait

your mind wonders
if this is your plight
this constant fight for your life.

The hardest part of depression is trying to stay positive

The best thing for depression is to try to stay positive

A double edge sword

and

All I'm doing is trying to keep my head above water.

I know heartache and I know pain
Knocking on heaven's door
thrust back onto earth's floor

Dredging through a tunnel
of sadness and despair,
crawling back from the depths of hell.

~yet~

I know peace that passes
all understanding

Hope that the sun is going to rise
in the east and set in the west

There's joy in life.

You Are Not Defined By A Diagnosis

You can be happy despite of it
It cannot control you
You have a destiny
Knowledge is power
Your dreams can come true

--

It's ok to be yourself
It's ok to be sad
It's ok to be angry
It's ok to have a bad day
It's ok to have several bad days

Always Forgotten

There was a time where I felt invisible
life was moving, yet I stood still

Balled up in a corner
literally and figuratively

All the while, life continued,
except mine

Looking back,
I was never forgotten
life did continue,
It was me.

*The will of my soul keeps me going
while my mind plays games at times.*

*I will not succumb to depression or
stay on edge with anxiety.*

*My will to defeat my inner thoughts
shall continue to prevail and be the
guiding light which shines towards my destiny.*

You have a place on this earth.
Your existence is immeasurable.
Don't give into the sadness.
Don't give into the pain.

-Stay-

Believe me when I tell you -
you would miss out on so much joy.

You have dreams and aspirations,
don't ever give up.

Poetic renditions
beautiful voices

Your hand covers mine,
theatrical display

Our eyes meet
the soprano high-
words are unnecessary

Love cries out in song from the stage,
love cries out in the mezzanine.

*There may be storms in your life and
you may have to search for your peace.*

*There's so much life outside yourself,
look at your beautiful surroundings.*

*Take in that ocean breeze,
watch the waves crash against the shore.*

Focus.

Take a look around you and, just be.

You never know where you're headed,
if you're headed in the right direction or not.

You have to keep doing your best
and being the best that you can.

Treat others with respect,
show kindness and compassion.

Work hard at whatever your dream is
and, have hope that it will come true.

When you wake to witness the sunrise,
notice the warmth of the sun upon
your face as it envelops your body

Remember how blessed you truly are -
as another day is not promised

Love a little harder.
Forgive a little more.

Let go of the past and
live your best life.

My Love

Moonlight through the window
reaching in the night
sweet face
gentle kisses
soft words
strong hands

-Eternally yours-

Mental illness is raw and ugly,
it's about fighting to keep
your head above water.

Keep fighting
fight for you,
fight for your future.

Waves crashing beyond the shore
tears into the sea
I am lost, please find me.

--

Insignificant and invisible,
yet no one could see
the darkness that overwhelms me.

*When you get "so close" and start to see the
light at the end of the tunnel.*

*You reach and you keep reaching, but
the light seems further and further away.*

It becomes this cat and mouse game.

You are tired of the bullshit – tired of the game.

Don't be embarrassed of your mental health,
your insecurities or doubts,
your need to reach out

This life is not easy at times.
It's ok to not be ok.
It's ok to not be positive all the time.
It's ok to take a break.

It's ok.

When your struggles seem too great and
you think you can't go on,

Look towards the sky
feel the sun upon your face
know in that moment, you matter

Keep hope alive in your heart
your strength will get you through.

This too will pass.

*The fright of your life is when your
child isn't quite right.*

*News that brings you to your knees,
the innocence you know is lost
to a diagnosis and loss of dreams.*

*Grasping for hope and finding faith,
humbled that you are all she has and
the realization that life will continue.*

*I don't have all the answers
I don't have it all figured out
I don't profess to know it all*

*I know that we can be
there for one another,
while we try to figure it out.*

*Devouring their prey, blood dripping
from the corners of their mouths,
ripping the flesh of the sacrificial lamb*

*Howling into the night, pleased with
themselves and their catch.*

*Bellies full, their lies and deceit
met with a sense of pride.*

Yet, it wasn't the wolves.

Guard me from the pain of the past.
Lift me beyond this tumultuous life.
Shield me from this cruel world.
Let me find peace in your embrace.

Take me with you.
Shelter me.
Give me hope.
Remind me of who I am.

Gift me this.

*Blue skies, ocean breeze
salt lingering in the air
ebb and flow of the waves.*

*Serenity, my sanity.
Quieting my soul.*

*I call out into the darkness
as it suffocates me at times.*

*It's just me and God,
and I pray.*

*He's heard it all,
there's really not much to say.*

*On a wing and a prayer,
somehow, I get through.*

*He gifts me with a sunrise, so
bright and so true.*

We do this dance, he and I.

*The cold wind blows
when you walk into the room.*

*The warmth dissipates as the
chill permeates to the bone.*

Darkness has arrived.

An angel sent from above,
in her splendor and grace
to keep you from harm,
to keep you safe.

Whispers your name
calling out like the breeze,
waiting beside you
in times of need.

Just one prayer away.

If you've had a rough day, week, year or life:

There may be a cloud overhead
raining sadness down on you.

Please know that the sun
is shining over the horizon.

There is a light at the
end of the tunnel.

Hope is right there,
waiting for you to grasp it.

The tears overflow
as I turn the pages of
the memories in my mind,
the good and the bad-
which sum up this life I've lived.

Reminiscing.

Silence Kept Under Wraps:

Tumultuous emotions shrouded,
hidden from view, mind clouded.

A pain too great to share,
it's too much for most to bear.

Some things are better left unsaid,
these feelings trapped within my head.

Darkness summons you to stay within it,
to remain hidden.

Don't be deceived,
you come from light.

You are light and love.

You shine so bright,
even when you don't
realize it - you do.

I've been in that darkness, I survived.

If you need a hand, take mine.

The signs
are loud and clear.

As I lay in silence,
I was dying inside.

Nobody asked,
like nobody cared.

As the sun rises in the east,
there's hope.

Blue skies and the warmth of the sun,
there's joy.

The people that never leave in times of need,
that's love.

Blessings bestowed on you,
is happiness.

Your existence is vital, it has meaning.

Your life is a gift.

Searching for something –
anything, to replace this darkness.

I find joy in a photo
of a place I'll never
witness, I'll never see.

Blue skies, blue water,
a serene scene.

Renewing the soul, even temporarily.

*My heart heavy, you want me to talk
I can see your eyes glaze over.*

*Instantly, I don't want to talk,
you aren't deserving of my thoughts.*

*I know you will chastise me,
I can see it in your eyes,
hear it in your voice.*

My feelings are not misplaced, they are valid.

A rendezvous with death,
the crackling in my lungs
with every breath.

I stood there, amongst the
flames, fire spreading all
around me.

A fire I couldn't contain,
I couldn't contain the flame.

I sprung up from my slumber,
not my time, not my number.

When life breaks you and
you question how to proceed,
a strength emerges that you didn't
realize you had.

This inner strength lies dormant
until your soul cries out,
a will to survive rushes through you.

This is the strength
that will make you whole.

As the curtain closes,
the cabaret of emotions
on full display.

No longer hidden
behind a façade.

Alone, the tears fall ...
tears that were caught
up in your throat,

Freely fall.

A mirror does not depict one's true self,
a reflection of "imperfections"

Truth lies in the soul,
where past experiences and
inner thoughts shed light
in a sacred space hidden from most.

Bodies age, but the soul is timeless.

I quiet my mind
I need peace in my life

I know what's going on,
I don't take a blind eye
to the world or worldly events,

I want peace
I pray for that
I pray for equality

I can whisper love and hope
I can offer support, but
I can't let hate in my space.

I won't forget that moment,
the date etched on my heart as a reminder.

I lost a part of myself that day
~oh, but what I gained~
A will to thrive and survive.

Most importantly,
I found peace.

My Shadow

When darkness befalls,
she's dancing on the wall

my protected inner child,
happy and carefree with a
freedom to just be

unaffected by the difficulties
of this world

innocent and naive to strife,
living a seemingly sheltered life

and

somehow, she's me.

The foundation laid,
the roots take hold.

I shouldn't worry,
I'm golden, I'm good.

My feet got knocked out
from underneath me.

I've lost my footing,
I've fallen, you see.

I stand back up,
I try again –
I'll keep doing that,
again and again.

Unless you've been through it,
unless you've seen it first-hand,
you'll never fully understand.

It won't stop,
I can't wish it away,
it's burned in my mind for eternity.

I fight back,
it won't break me.

I'm too strong for that.

Just hang on:
for one more day
for one more night.

Search for the little joys in life.

Find one thing that gives you joy today,
tomorrow find one more thing.

Keep putting one foot in front of the other,
step by step,
day by day.

Don't give up.

The End

About the Author

Jami Kellett is a mental health
advocate and suicide survivor.
Her purpose is to contribute
to suicide prevention
and encourage others
to choose life.

You can find her on:

Twitter at: JustJami@jamingeorge04 or
Instagram at: jamik1068.

Have a seat and watch the sunrise with her sometime.

Acknowledgments

Twitter's Writing Community:

Your expertise and support are completely overwhelming. Without all of you, I wouldn't have pursued my dream of writing and, for that I am grateful. Where in the world can you have direct access to incredible writers, authors and poets, but on Twitter? Nowhere.

These are my people, they have blessed me beyond words - their presence is a gift, **give them a follow***:*

Editor:
Nancy W- @Nancywaddell18

Formatting:
Barry Brunswick - @BarrySBrunswick

Designer of My Book Cover:

Robert R. Fike - @robfike

Beta Readers:
Tawnee Cowen - @findmeintheend
Missie - @MattMissie

Liz - @Ltward2
Dr. Victoria Rose - @VW7772
Michael Stoneburner - @evilgeniustobe
Granny Rock - @JudyDFerrell1
J.D. Greyson - @JDGreysonwrites
David Middleham - @DavidMiddleham
Aspen Brave - @Write2Fite
James C. Glass - @JamesCGlass1
Franka - @fjhaddley
Amanda -@amandajk
Jacqueline - @JaysQuill
Poetkisses @poetkisses
Migs - @OminousHallways
Jana - @janalynnjenks

Just Jenny - @JennyHayut
Lisa M - @LisaM_soundz
Rebecca Ridge - @AuthorRidge
Keturah - @KeturahBarchers
F khend - @Fed_2001
Dr. Jessica @drjessica17
Veil @veil_lord
Cathalina - @cathalina1972
Dr. Maggie Gilewicz - @MaggieGilewicz
MissieDee - @MissieDeeDee
Stephen @GallifreyGamgee
Kathryn Inman @kathryninman9
Melissa Rea - @author_rea
DeeDee - @leopardladyy53
Magnolia - @magnolia3169
David - @d_ast777
Brian - @brianwilliamco
Tony Anderson - @TonyThePoett
Dzintra - @DzintraSullivan
Buki - @bkshittu
Katrina Lippolis - @kitkatpoetess
MJM - @MikeJMele
Melanie - @mwhitock93
Melanie @Melanie_Korach
Just Rie - @gftomatoes
Jerry T - @JerryT85373
Tanvi @TheTanviSingh

Printed in Great Britain
by Amazon

65579744R00081